Caleigh

Presented to

The Yosts

Presented by

July 2012

Date

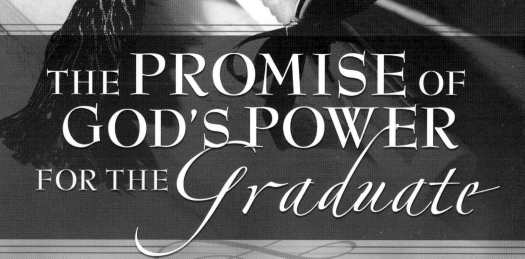

THE PROMISE OF GOD'S POWER
FOR THE *Graduate*

Meditations of

Strength, Courage, and Wisdom

for the Great Adventure of Life

SPIRIT PRESS

The Promise of God's Power for the Graduate
ISBN 1-40372-037-1

Published in 2006 by Spirit Press, an imprint of Dalmatian Press, LLC.
Copyright © 2006 Dalmatian Press, LLC. Franklin, Tennessee 37067.

Scripture quotations marked CEV are from *The Contemporary English Version*.
Copyright © 1991, 1992, 1995 by American Bible Society. Used by permission.

Scripture quotations marked GNT are from the *Good News Translation, Second Edition*,
Copyright © 1992 by American Bible Society. Used by permission. All rights reserved.

Scripture quotations marked MSG are taken from *The Message*. Copyright © by Eugene
H. Peterson, 1993, 1994, 1995. Used by permission of NavPress Publishing Group.

Scripture quotations marked NASB are taken from the *New American Standard Bible*.
Copyright © The Lockman Foundation 1960, 1962, 1963, 1968, 1971, 1972, 1973, 1975,
1977, 1995. Used by permission.

Scripture quotations marked NIrV are from the *Holy Bible, New International Reader's
Version™*, Copyright © 1995, 1996, 1998 by International Bible Society. Used by
permission of Zondervan Publishing House. All rights reserved.

Scripture quotations marked NIV are taken from the *Holy Bible, New International
Version®*. NIV®. Copyright © 1973, 1978, 1984 by International Bible Society.
Used by permission of Zondervan Publishing House. All rights reserved.

Scripture quotations marked NKJV are taken from *The New King James Version*.
Copyright © 1979, 1980, 1982, Thomas Nelson, Inc.

Scripture quotations marked NLT are taken from the *Holy Bible, New Living
Translation*, Copyright © 1996. Used by permission of Tyndale House Publishers, Inc.,
Wheaton, Illinois 60189. All rights reserved.

Scripture quotations marked NRSV are from *The New Revised Standard Version of the
Bible*, Copyright © 1989, 1997 by The Division of Christian Education of the National
Council of the Churches of Christ in the USA. Used by permission. All rights reserved.

Editor: Lila Empson
Writer: P. Barnhart
Text Designer: Whisner Design Group

06 07 08 09 WAI 10 9 8 7 6 5 4 3 2 1

14951

You will hear a voice say,

"This is the way; turn around

and walk here."

Isaiah 30:21 NLT

Contents

Introduction

You have come to an end that is a beginning. You don't have to go back and try to make a brand-new start, because you can start now and make a brand-new end. What you hope to become and who you want to be begin now. The page before you is blank, awaiting the impressions of your dreams and dares. You will arrive later by starting now.

Nothing is more important to the rest of your life than the first step into it. Step boldly with faith and confidence. Take long strides of vision and ambition. Find the high road and walk there. Take as your companions those who share your goals and principles. As you go through the open door, feel God's presence in your heart and at your side. God wants to help you with your new beginning. Pick up your

pen, and God will guide the hand with which you write. God will help you page by page, chapter by chapter. He will give you information to write and inspiration with which to write it.

Those are God's promises to you. He will give you power for the first step, and for all the steps that come after it. You will truly know the power of God's promises.

Hear Opportunity Knock

*I have placed before you an
open door that no one can shut.*

Revelation 3:8 NIV

As you move forward from graduation, you will
not be short of opportunities. They will knock on your
door every day. Sometimes you will readily recognize
your opportunities because they will knock loudly.
"Here I am!" they will say. For instance, you might
become aware of a job position that fits both your
preparation and your passion. Or you might meet a
new friend, and the commonality you share with that
person indicates a progressive and profitable path you
can walk together.

But other times opportunity knocks softly. It comes
as quiet innuendo and gives whispering hints of possibility and promise. It arrives wrapped in a plan A that
doesn't work out, but behind it is a plan B that is better.
Not infrequently, opportunity shows up in some person

who puts a gentle hand on your shoulder and turns you toward a horizon you have not seen. Opportunity comes from God, and God puts it everywhere.

Whether opportunity comes boldly or comes in subtle ways, listen for its knock so you will know when it has arrived. Keep the locks off the doors. Do not turn away from what heaven sends. Do not focus so much on safety and security that you miss hearing opportunity announce itself. Focus on possibilities, not on problems. Be always aware that opportunities are often small doors that open into large rooms.

Hear opportunities knock on your door, and thank God for knowing when to send them to you. Grasp them with a grateful heart.

> Dear God,
> I praise you for blessing me with so many
> gifts, opportunities, and possibilities.
> Amen.

Far Down the Field

Whether we are at home or away,
we make it our aim to please him.

2 Corinthians 5:9 NRSV

As you set targets and objectives for the future, aim far. Erect goalposts way down the field, and establish markers along the way to note and measure progress. Plan long-range, and work stage by stage toward the end. You will cross the finish line if it is strung tightly and brightly across the lane of your endeavors. You will get out of the starting blocks quickly and sustain your stride when the goal is vividly before you.

It is said that when Margaret Mitchell wrote her renowned *Gone With the Wind*, she wrote the last chapter first to give herself a goal to strive toward. She wrote her newspaper columns the same way. She knew where she was going before heading out. The last line called forth all the others. Where she wanted to end indicated where she would begin and how she would

continue. Means developed out of ends. New thoughts and fresh expressions emerged along the way in order that the goal might be reached.

As you go through life, always be running toward something. Set goals that act as magnets pulling you toward your dreams. How hard you work and how well you perform depend on how far you plan to go. Additionally, long-range objectives keep you from getting frustrated over short-term failures and defeats. Knowing your goal and where it is also enables you to act formidably against the goalies you encounter along the way.

Periodically affirming where you want to end generates ingenuity and determination. Putting up targets is the first step toward accomplishment and achievement.

> *Dear God,*
> *speak to me that I may know what you want*
> *me to do with my life. May my objectives and*
> *goals be those you have in mind for me.*
> *Amen.*

The Promises of God

We were ready to share with you not only the Good News from God but even our own lives. You were so dear to us!

1 Thessalonians 2:8 GNT

*I am standing at the door, knocking; if you hear
my voice and open the door, I will come in to you,
and eat with you, and you with me.*

Revelation 3:20 NRSV

*You will learn what is right and honest and fair.
From these, an ordinary person can learn to be smart,
and young people can gain knowledge and good sense.*

Proverbs 1:3–4 CEV

*You have done many good things for me, LORD. . . .
I believe in your commands; now teach
me good judgment and knowledge.*

Psalm 119:65–66 NLT

*To all who received him, who believed in his name,
he gave power to become children of God,
who were born, not of blood or of the will
of the flesh or of the will of man, but of God.*

John 1:12–13 NRSV

Living the Promises

It seems to me that we often, almost sulkily,
reject the good that God offers us because, at
the moment, we expect some other good.

C. S. Lewis

To be what you are, and to become what you are
capable of becoming, it is the only end of life.

Robert Louis Stevenson

Happiness is something that comes
into our lives through doors we don't
even remember leaving open.

Rose Wilder Lane

Education is the process of helping everyone
discover their uniqueness, develop that
uniqueness, and share it with others.

Max Lucado

Thank God every morning when you get up that
you have something to do that day which must
be done, whether you like it or not.

Charles Kingsley

The Future Is Coming

Listen to advice and accept instruction,
that you may gain wisdom for the future.
Proverbs 19:20 NRSV

Pick up your telescope and aim it at the future.
Look around the corner, down the road, and up the
mountain. Envision what lies ahead of you. Dream of
good things. Gaze at what you will achieve. See what
God has in store for you. Believe that what God has in
store for you is even better than what is or what has
been. Know you are created and built for the future.

Your future is bright, and it is coming. Look
through your telescope and you will see the future getting closer and closer. It rushes in your direction, eager
to meet you and enter into partnership with you. It
wants to know who you are, what you think, what your
plans are. The future is interested in the purpose of
your life, and the principles by which you intend to live
out the purpose. It is interested in how you understand
your resources and what you think of your abilities.

The future wants to know how big a part God will play in your pursuits and endeavors.

See the horizon God has set before you. That is your future, and it belongs to you. It is your space and time in which to live freely and fully. And it is here.

Your future begins right now. For a long time and with great loving care, God has been getting it ready. It is his gift to you.

Thank you, dear God,
for my future that comes to me at
the rate of sixty minutes an hour.
Amen.

Work to Do

Hard work always pays off; mere
talk puts no bread on the table.

Proverbs 14:23 MSG

Graduation means it is time to get busy. It is time to put your mind around the challenges of the future, your hands on the tasks in front of you, and your heart in the direction you are going. It is time to accept tough jobs as a challenge and reach for the ability you have to get them done. Your future won't be what you want it to be by accident. It will be what you want it to be by work. It is time to work harder than you ever have before. What distinguishes a talented individual from a successful individual is a lot of hard work.

It is incredible how much you accomplish when you get busy doing it. When you put your hand to the wheel, you will make progress down the road. You will also have great joy and deep peace. An Amish farmer rebuked his son for being slow at doing his chores. He said, "God made the body to be used, my son. If you sit

around all day, you can't expect rest for your soul at night." Hard work honors God, who worked to make the world. When you do your work diligently, God rewards you with contentment and peace.

Your work expresses who you are and what you stand for. It is a mirror that reflects your effort, intention, and purpose.

Dear God,
thank you for helping me express myself
and give glory to you through my work.
Amen.

Seven Statements
of Affirmation

I Will ...

1. Be grateful for my education.

2. Appreciate and be thankful for my teachers.

3. Appreciate and be thankful for my parents.

4. Thank God for my abilities.

5. Know there's room for improvement.

6. Make definite plans for the future.

7. Never underestimate myself.

What I Need to Do...

____1. Write at least one teacher a letter of appreciation.

____2. Tell my parents what they mean to me.

____3. Read a book that challenges me.

____4. Visit a website that challenges me.

____5. Talk with a pastor about my future.

____6. Spend time with an ambitious friend my age.

____7. Spend time with a neighbor I admire.

Helping Others Helps You

His name was Fleming, and he was a poor farmer living in Ayrshire, Scotland, trying to scratch out a living for himself and his family on a few acres of depleted land. One day, while on the backside of his property, he heard a frantic cry for help coming from a nearby bog. He immediately dropped the reins of his plow horse and ran in the direction of the bog. The screams grew louder, and he ran faster. Getting to the bog, he saw a young boy mired in black muck up to his waist; the boy was screaming and trying to free himself from the quagmire. Farmer Fleming ran to him, jerked off his own shirt, twisted it into a rope, and thrust it to the young boy. He pulled him out of the slimy sludge onto dry and safe ground and then took him home to clean him up and send him on his grateful way.

He did not come to be served. Instead, he came to serve others.
Matthew 20:28 NIrV

The next day, a fancy carriage came to the Scotsman's modest farmhouse. An elegantly dressed nobleman stepped out and introduced himself as the father of the boy that Farmer Fleming had saved. The nobleman was most appreciative and said, "I want to repay you." The farmer said he couldn't accept payment for what he had done and waved off the offer. The nobleman persisted: "But you saved my son's life. If you hadn't done what you did, we would be burying him in two days." The farmer refused again and, just then, his own son came to the door to see what was going on. He was one of ten children. "Is that your boy?" asked the noble-man. "Yes," the farmer replied. "How old is he?" He was the same age as the nobleman's son. "Okay," the nobleman said, "I'll make a deal with you. If you won't take any pay from me, I promise to provide your son any level of education my son will be able to have. Whatever my boy can have, your boy can have." The farmer agreed to the arrangement, probably thinking it would never come about.

But the nobleman was good on his word and provided the very best schools for the farmer's son. As a student, he excelled at every level. Eventually, he entered Saint Mary's Medical School, London University, and graduated with top honors. It was there he began the research that led him to the discovery of penicillin, a discovery that changed the world. He served throughout World War I as a captain in the Army Medical Corps and, after the war, returned to Saint Mary's where he was a professor of great distinction. He was later knighted Sir Alexander Fleming and, in 1945, won the Nobel Prize for Medicine.

Years later, the same nobleman's son who was saved from the bog by Farmer Fleming was stricken with a severe case of pneumonia. He would have died had it not been for the drug discovered by the rescued boy. The nobleman's son, Randolph Churchill, did not die and lived to have a son of his own. The ability, dedication, and passion of that son steered nations through a treacherous war and defied a murderous tyrant. History will never forget Winston Churchill.

As you go out to make a contribution to the world, be helpful to others. Care about people and serve their needs. Don't seek rewards. The reward for a good deed is to have done it. Nevertheless, it is God's intention to bless you for what you do. Some of these blessings you won't recognize until you look back on your life, but they will be there. Whatever you put into life, it will come back to you. Everything balances out, like an equation you learn in school.

The mother of the great singer Marian Anderson worked long and hard as a domestic to make it possible for her daughter to pursue a singing career. The happiest day in Marian Anderson's life was not when Toscanini acclaimed her a "voice that comes once in a century." The happiest day was when she was able to come home after signing a long-term contract and say to her mother, "Mom, you can stop working now." At that moment, her mother, with tears of pride running down her face, knew all those years of hard work had paid off.

Life is a boomerang. Your good deeds return, sooner or later, with astounding accuracy. You reap what you sow. The things you do come back to you. They know the way.

Think Big

*Whenever you plant your crops, the Lord will send rain
to make them grow and will give you a rich harvest.*
Isaiah 30:23 GNT

As you enter the future, your strongest asset is
optimism. Take with you the high spirit of expectation.
Go forth, confident of your potential. Know that God
matches his steps to your cadence. Believe your ability,
trust your competence, and affirm God's power as your
strength. When one door closes, move your eyes away
from it, because one more suitable and pertinent is
opening. Through that door is the possibility for you to
give of yourself, utilize your talent, and make a difference in the world.

Think big. No one ever caught lions by setting
mousetraps. To catch lions, think in terms of lions and
not of mice. Set your aim high and reach for the sky.
The farther you reach, the farther you will go. Shoot
for the moon. If you miss, you'll still land among the
stars. Remember, when setting your sights on goals,

that God is your partner in what you want to do. If God is your partner, make your plans big. When you and God work together, potential increases and possibilities expand.

Dream big dreams, and watch them come true. When you face difficulties, look beyond them to opportunities. Think positively, and be enthusiastic about your thoughts. Put your thoughts into action and sustain them with an all-out effort. Tell God about your goals and why you want to reach them. Invite God's power into everything you do.

You can achieve more and go farther with a positive attitude. As you go forth in confidence, God goes forth with you in strength and power. The two of you go together.

I will think positively, dear God, and I will positively think. I will believe in what I want to see, and I will see it. Amen.

Make Plans

*David gave his son Solomon the plans for the portico
of the temple, its buildings, its storerooms, its upper parts,
its inner rooms and the place of atonement.*

1 Chronicles 28:11 NIV

Making plans is a key to successful action. Clearly
knowing what you want to do and how you want to do
it gets you moving toward your goals. What you plan
ahead has clearer directions for beginning and greater
endurance for getting there. To get to where you want
to be, design a plan in your mind and follow the plan.

God modeled long-range planning. Jesus came
down through forty-two generations. For all that time,
God planned to come to earth. What he wanted to do
was important enough to plan that far ahead. No
amount of preparation would be too much to reach
such a goal. Preparation is essential to you in reaching
your goals. You will get to where you want to be not by
chance but by preparation. You will, in fact, find out
that the more you prepare, the luckier you are. Select
your goal, prepare to reach it, and get going toward it.

Success is the result of making plans and carrying them out. Just as important as the will to succeed is the will to *plan* to succeed. It was said of Winston Churchill that his seemingly impromptu speeches had been written well in advance. An important key to success is self-confidence, and self-confidence comes from being prepared.

Planning brings the future into the present so something can be done about it now. It plows ground in which you and God plant seed and, together, look forward to the harvest.

Dear God,
before I was born you made
plans for me. Guide me as
I make plans for myself.
Amen.

The Promises of God

*You have given up your old way of life with its habits.
Each of you is now a new person. You are becoming more
and more like your Creator. . . . God loves you and has
chosen you as his own special people.*

Colossians 3:9–10, 12 CEV

*I thank my God upon every remembrance of you, always
in every prayer of mine making request for you all with joy,
for your fellowship in the gospel from the first day until
now, being confident of this very thing, that He who has
begun a good work in you will complete it.*

Philippians 1:3–6 NKJV

*Kindle afresh the gift of God which is in you through the
laying on of my hands. For God has not given us a spirit
of timidity, but of power and love and discipline.*

2 Timothy 1:6–7 NASB

*Concentrate on doing your best for God, work you won't be
ashamed of, laying out the truth plain and simple.*

2 Timothy 2:15 MSG

Living the Promises

Optimism is essential to achievement and is also
the foundation of courage and of true progress.

Nicholas Murray Butler

Among those whom I like or admire, I can find
no common denominator, but among those I
love, I can: all of them make me laugh.

W. H. Auden

There is always music amongst the trees in the
garden, but our hearts must be very
quiet to hear it.

Minnie Aumonier

The block of granite which was an obstacle in
the path of the weak becomes a stepping-stone
in the path of the strong.

Thomas Carlyle

Have a love affair with yourself. Until you have
a love affair with you, you can't begin to have
as much fun as there is with somebody else.

Viki King

You Are Gifted

*God has given each of us the ability
to do certain things well.*
Romans 12:6 NLT

You have what it takes. You are not shortchanged in the ability department. The competence for what you want to do is within you. It is good, rich, and potent. It is sharp, steadfast, and sure. When what you have inside yourself goes outside yourself, it is fantastic!

There is something more important than ability, and that is the ability to recognize ability. Recognize your ability. Call it by name and claim that it belongs to you. You are designed for accomplishment. You are engineered for achievement. Acknowledge your capacity and capability. Be aware of what you are able to do. Use your skills and talents. When you use them, they become treasures that bless you and others.

Acknowledge that God has gifted you. Don't shy away from your endowment in some sort of false humility or feigned inability. Don't be like the man who dreamed about arriving in heaven and seeing a giant Christmas tree loaded with presents. When he inquired what that meant, he was told those were all the gifts he turned down that God tried to give him on earth.

Receive the gifts God gives you. Receive them, take a close look at them, and believe they are good. Don't be afraid of your own gifts.

Dear God,
thank you for endowing me so richly.
I am much, deeply, and often blessed.
Amen.

Power Not Your Own

The name of the LORD is a strong tower;
the righteous run to it and are safe.
Proverbs 18:10 NIV

You don't have to do what you have to do by
yourself. There is an outside dynamic available to you
for all your goals, tasks, and responsibilities. No journey you make or path you take has to be made or taken
alone. You will never have to sing solo. God will add
his voice to yours in all productions and performances.
You will never have to row with both oars. God will
take one of them in his capable hands and pull in
rhythm with your effort. At no time will it be necessary
for you to scale a mountain by yourself. God will tie
himself to you and the two of you will climb in tandem.
There will always be two sets of footprints on the
beach, one right beside the other.

You will never have to sit at the table of decision
alone. God will sit with you as guide and consultant.
Whatever advice you need, God will give. Whatever

insight will help, God will provide. No matter how many opponents you have to fight to reach your goal, God will wield mighty weapons of authority and power on your behalf. God makes available what you need for what you desire to accomplish. You can count on God's help at all times and in all things.

In all endeavors, you and God are a team. Whatever your business, God is your partner in it. You never work alone. You never walk alone.

*Dear God,
because of you I am never alone,
always accompanied, and for that
I am most grateful.
Amen.*

Seven Statements
of Affirmation

I Will ...

1. Believe I am able to do what I need to do because God is with me.

2. Call on others and let them help me.

3. Be open to fresh ideas and new methods.

4. Be aware of God's presence in all things.

5. Change direction when it is necessary to do so.

6. Keep my sense of humor when disappointments come.

7. Give God my time and attention each day.

What I Need to Do ...

___ 1. Make a list of what I hope to have accomplished one year from now.

___ 2. Make Sunday worship a regular habit.

___ 3. Join a group of encouraging people.

___ 4. Send a thank-you e-mail to someone today.

___ 5. Make a financial donation to a charitable cause.

___ 6. Find someone who needs my help and give it.

___ 7. Plan to learn something new each day.

Sharpening Stones

We also boast of our troubles, because we know that trouble produces endurance, endurance brings God's approval, and his approval creates hope.

Romans 5:3–4 GNT

Troubles and difficulties are the sharpening stones by which you become more competent. Adversity introduces you to yourself, to what you feel and think and know. It enables you to say hello to your aspirations and determinations. Bad times get you in touch with what it takes to plow through to good times.

English poet John Milton is a good example. When he turned fifty, his world came crashing down. As a supporter of Cromwell, he had been given a post in the government, but when the monarchy came back to power in England, Milton lost his job. His second wife died in childbirth, as had his first. His oldest daughter became disabled, and he was going blind. John Milton decided to forgo public life and work on that epic poem he had for a long time dreamed of writing. He finished

Paradise Lost in 1665, the year of the Great Plague in London, which was followed by the Great Fire of 1666. Persevering, Milton managed to find a publisher whose presses were spared by the flames. Despite all his hardships, or perhaps because of them, he sold the manuscript and it became the great classic it is today.

Henry Wadsworth Longfellow knew what he was talking about when he said that sometimes "the lowest ebb is the turn of the tide."

Adversity breeds toughness. The tough survive, and succeed. You grow through what you go through. Whatever or whenever it is, God goes through it with you.

> *Dear God,*
> *thank you for bad times that wake me*
> *up to the good stuff I wasn't paying*
> *attention to.*
> *Amen.*

Better Than a Plan

*I cry to God Most High, to God
who fulfills his purpose for me.*

Psalm 57:2 NRSV

Having graduated, you need a plan for the rest of your life. You need a schedule for getting from one point to another, a design that traces the journey for you. As important as a plan is, there is something more essential. You need a purpose. God has something better than a wonderful plan for your life. God has a superlative purpose for your life. Without a great purpose to make a good plan necessary, you may get somewhere and discover it's not the place you want to be. With a solid purpose, you will get to where God wants you to be when God wants you to be there.

Three stonemasons were once asked what they were doing. One said, "I'm cutting this stone." Another replied, "I'm earning my pay." The third got the answer right when he said, "I'm building a cathedral." Be good, but be good for something special in your life.

Be active, but make your activity serve God's purpose for you. Use your skill, talent, and ability to move through life toward the goal of God's rationale for who you are. You have a great purpose. You need a plan, but your purpose is much more important.

Whatever you have, know who gave it to you and why you have it. Use it to honor, glorify, love, and serve God.

As I seek and find my purpose in
life, dear God, may I be responsible,
honorable, and useful.
Amen.

A Graduate's Prayer

Dear God,
Thank you for loving me,
And wanting me to love you.
Thank you for knowing me,
And letting me know you.
Thank you for walking with me,
And talking with me as you do.
Thank you for what has been,
And for what is yet to come.
Thank you for wanting me on your side,
And for being on mine.
Amen.

Thoughts and Promises
for the Journey

*In all these things we are more than conquerors through him
who loved us. For I am convinced that neither death nor life,
neither angels nor demons, neither the present nor the future . . .
will be able to separate us from the love of God
that is in Christ Jesus our Lord.*

Romans 8:37–39 NIV

Have regular hours for work and play;
make each day both useful and pleasant,
and prove that you understand the
worth of time by employing it well.

Louisa May Alcott

*More than anything else, put God's work first and do what he
wants. Then the other things will be yours as well. Don't worry
about tomorrow. It will take care of itself.*

Matthew 6:33–34 CEV

The glories of the moment will inspire the
hour; the victories of the morning will
embolden the day; the triumphs of the
present will shape the future.

Author Unknown

Bigger Than You Think

*You will receive power when the
Holy Spirit has come upon you.*
Acts 1:8 NRSV

William Wilberforce was responsible for abolishing slavery in England. He fought a long and arduous battle for two decades. Again and again, businessmen who didn't want to lose cheap labor put up money to defeat proposals Wilberforce made to Parliament. He endured defeat after defeat, sometimes coming so close to winning he could almost taste it.

The multiple losses left Wilberforce discouraged, but he plowed on toward the goal of freedom for all people. He sometimes became depressed, but he would pull himself out of the pit to get on the road again. Wilberforce was determined to see the end of slave trade in his country. His favorite scripture was Galatians 6:9, which says to not "grow weary in doing what is right" (NRSV). In 1807 the tide turned, and Parliament voted to abolish the slave trade.

William Wilberforce won the battle but, at five feet tall, he was a most unlikely battler. You are bigger than you think you are. You can influence the outcome of projects and issues you thought you'd have to leave to others. You can put your name on accomplishments you were certain someone else would have to sign. You can do more in your life than you have projected in your most ambitious dreams. You are able.

You and God will stand in the winner's circle because, together, you have what it takes to win the race. You are a team that can't be beaten.

> *Thank you, dear God,*
> *for endowing me in such rich,*
> *vital, and varied ways. I am*
> *overwhelmed by your blessings.*
> *Amen.*

Music in the Storm

He calmed the storm to a whisper and stilled the waves.
Psalm 107:29 NLT

There is a legend that tells of a German baron who, at his castle on the Rhine, stretched wires from tower to tower so that the winds might create a harp-like instrument and make beautiful music. Soft and gentle breezes came and played their touch upon the baron's creation, but no music was born. Then, one dark and ominous night, a treacherous storm of assailing wind and assaulting rain arose as a great tempest and came thundering down upon the castle in a mighty fury. The baron went out to the edge of his castle to assess the damage, and it was then he heard his harp filling the air with strains of beautiful melody that drowned out the tumult of the storm.

Sometimes, as you go through life, it will be the tempest that brings out your best and most profound music. Your antagonist will actually turn out to be your

helper; someone who opposes you will provide the stimulation you need to get ahead. It was in the wilderness that Jesus got ready for the Cross, and it was the Cross that unleashed the Resurrection and produced forever after life. Each conflict or crisis you experience is homework that prepares you to pass examinations that will come. The oak is both tested and toughened by the storm. And the most brilliant colors of plants are found on the highest mountains, in spots exposed to the wildest and worst of weather.

Most of the shining lights of history were made so by their struggle with either some disability or some responsibility that seemed too great for their powers.

> *Dear God,*
> *thank you for the songs of faith you*
> *give me to sing and sing to me*
> *during the storms of life.*
> *Amen.*

The Promises of God

Seek your happiness in the LORD; and he will give you your heart's desire. Give yourself to the LORD; trust in him, and he will help you.

Psalm 37:4–5 GNT

Trust in the LORD with all your heart, and lean not on your own understanding; in all your ways acknowledge Him, and He shall direct your paths.

Proverbs 3:5–6 NKJV

This same God who takes care of me will supply all your needs from his glorious riches, which have been given to us in Christ Jesus.

Philippians 4:19 NLT

If you diligently obey the LORD your God, being careful to do all His commandments which I command you today, the LORD your God will set you high above all the nations of the earth. All these blessings will come upon you and overtake you if you obey the LORD your God.

Deuteronomy 28:1–2 NASB

Living the Promises

There is a weightlessness to life with no
regrets. Bear no grudges and welcome
others with a glad heart.

Author Unknown

A man should keep his little brain stocked with
all the furniture that he is likely to use, and the
rest he can put away in the lumber room of his
library, where he can get to it if he wants it.

Arthur Conan Doyle

Whether or not our efforts are favored by life,
let us be able to say, when we near the great
goal, "I have done what I could."

Louis Pasteur

The weaker we feel, the harder we lean on God.
And the harder we lean, the stronger we grow.

Joni Eareckson Tada

Never undertake anything for which
you wouldn't have the courage to ask the
blessings of heaven.

Georg Christoph Lichtenberg

Older Than You

Even in old age they will still produce fruit;
they will remain vital and green.

Psalm 92:14 NLT

To be successful, consult people older than yourself. Those who came before you have been where
you're going and know the way. Pick their brains, and
add file after file to your own. Do a search through the
websites of their wisdom and greatly broaden the
capacity of your own system. Consult their memory
and move to the next level of your own understanding
and perception. Ask what they think, how they feel,
what they would do. People older than you have
answers waiting for your questions.

Those who have lived for some time may be short-
er in step, but they are longer in mind. They have aged
past limitations, restrictions, and inhibitions. They can
teach you where the shortcuts are and get you in touch
with the foundational bottom line. Traditional Japanese
belief affirms the wisdom of those who are older.

The longer one lives, the smarter one gets. In this long-standing tradition, there is a respect for older people that borders on reverence. Older people are honored, admired, and followed. Their advice is sought, taken, and used.

Stand on the shoulders of older people and you will see farther than if you remain on the flat ground of only your own experiences, or those of your peers.

Thank you, dear God, for those who have lived longer than I have, know more than I do, and have been where I haven't yet gone. Amen.

The Best Policy

My honesty will answer for me later, when you
come to look into my wages with you.
Genesis 30:33 NRSV

If the Greek philosopher Diogenes were still wandering around with a lantern looking for an honest person, would he be able to end his search at your door? As you go through your years as worker and citizen, be honest in all things. Guard against the slippery slope of dishonesty that descends into places you don't want to be. Meet everything head-on and honestly.

Cincinnati Reds pitcher Danny Graves lost his wallet at the start of a West Coast road trip and figured he'd never see it gain. The wallet contained credit cards, his driver's license, his identification card to get into ballparks, and $1,400 in cash. Imagine his surprise when the wallet was returned to him in the mail two days later. A man who cleaned the team bus in San Diego found it and not only returned the wallet but took extraordinary measures to ensure its safety during

shipping. He exchanged the cash for traveler's checks and wrote Graves a note that said, "I took $26 out to overnight it to you." The man sent his name, address, phone number, and wrote, "All I ask for is could you please sign an autograph for my father." Graves was more than glad to accommodate that request.

Tell the truth. The truth sets you free to be who you are supposed to be. An honest person is a blessing to everyone.

Dear God,
keep my mind clear about what is true
and what is not. Make me honest,
and keep me that way.
Amen.

Seven Statements
of Affirmation

I Will ...

1. Focus on possibilities, not problems.

2. Determine to succeed.

3. Have an honest point of view.

4. Control my attitude so it doesn't control me.

5. Find a way to turn bad news into good news.

6. Have a positive mental image of myself.

7. Be excited about my life.

What I Need to Do ...

____1. Interview three people who read a lot.

____2. Read a book written by a positive thinker.

____3. Watch the History Channel on television.

____4. Attend a play that makes me think.

____5. Write a statement of my basic beliefs.

____6. Play a challenging board game with friends.

____7. Have a friend who is smarter than I am.

What Goes Around
Comes Around

He almost didn't see the woman, stranded on the side of the road and standing beside her expensive automobile. The rain obscured his vision, and he nearly drove right by her. But

A stingy planter gets a stingy crop; a lavish planter gets a lavish crop.

2 Corinthians 9:6 MSG

good peripheral vision showed her to him, and he skidded his car to a stop about twenty yards in front of where she was. He waved his arms in warm greeting so she wouldn't be alarmed by his approach. Getting to where she stood soaked and weary,

he said, "Everything's going to be okay, ma'am. I'm here to help you." This assured her some. She mumbled words of gratitude through her clenched teeth, and began to relax a little. "Get in the car, out of the rain, and I'll take care of it," he said to her confidently. As she opened the door and slid her small body into a leather seat, he laughed and said, "Oh, by the way, my name's Garth."

All that was wrong with the car was a loose wire that had disconnected the power, and Garth reconnected it in no time. While under the hood, he checked out everything else and made a minor adjustment to one of the intake valves. As he walked around the car, the rain now gone, the woman rolled down the window to talk to him. She told him she was from a neighboring state and was passing through on the way to her daughter's in a town about two hundred miles down the road. Garth told her the car would work fine now, and she asked how much she owed him. Garth told her he wouldn't think of taking any money. When she insisted, he told her she could pay him back by doing something for the next person she saw who needed help. He waited until she drove off in her car, and headed home.

Twenty or so miles down the road, the woman saw a small café, and she suddenly felt hungry. Stress always made her hungry. She went into the café to get a sandwich and some hot coffee. She sat down at a corner table, and a waitress came over to take her order. Seeing the woman was wet, the waitress brought a towel so the woman could dry her hair. "Thank you so much; you're kind," the woman said to the smiling and pregnant waitress. The waitress said she was glad to be of some help and took the woman's order for a club sandwich and some coffee. When the woman finished the sandwich and after she drank a second cup of coffee, she got ready to pay her bill and leave. Looking in her purse, she discovered she had nothing smaller than a hundred-dollar bill. She asked the waitress if she could make change for that and was told she could.

As the waitress went to the cash register to get change, the woman remembered Garth and what he'd said about doing something for the next person she met who needed help. Surely this young, pregnant woman working in a roadside café could use some help, the woman thought to herself. She got up from the table and quickly left the café. The waitress, going back to the table with the change from the hundred-dollar bill, saw that the woman was not at the table and wondered where she could be. Then she noticed a note written on a napkin, under which there were six more one-hundred-dollar bills. "You don't owe me anything," the note said. "Somebody helped me out just a while ago, and now I want to help you." The young woman could certainly use the money, and her face flooded with tears. She couldn't believe such a thing had happened to her. Her first baby was due in about a month, the insurance wouldn't pay everything, and her husband had been out just that day looking for a better-paying job.

When she got home that evening and went through the door, her husband was in the kitchen getting supper ready. Knowing how worried he'd been about their finances, she put her arms around him and said, "Don't worry anymore, honey, everything's going to be okay." Then she hugged him tightly and said, "I love you so much, Garth."

When you give, you receive. What you sow, you reap. What goes around, comes around.

A Graduate's Prayer

Dear God,
Thank you for being
Behind me to encourage,
In front of me to invite,
Beside me to accompany,
Underneath me to support,
Above me to empower.
Thank you for everywhere you are
To love, accept, and guide me.
Amen.

Thoughts and Promises
for the Journey

You who stand here, chisels in hand, about
to hew out the future, have something inside
yourselves: humanity's most precious
mental gift—the eternal resilience,
the everlasting bounce in man.

William Allen White

Don't be afraid. I am with you. Don't
tremble with fear. I am your God.
I will make you strong, as I protect
you with my arm and give you victories.

Isaiah 41:10 CEV

The world cares little about what a man or
woman knows; it is what the man or woman
is able to do that counts.

Booker T. Washington

An education isn't how much you have
committed to memory, or even how much you
know. It's being able to differentiate between
what you know and what you don't. It's
knowing where to go to find out what you need
to know; and it's knowing how to use the
information you get.

William Feather

How You Respond

We are pressed on every side by troubles, but we are not crushed and broken. We are perplexed, but we don't give up and quit. We are hunted down, but God never abandons us. We get knocked down, but we get up again and keep going.

2 Corinthians 4:8–9 NLT

Your life will be about 20 percent of what happens to you and about 80 percent of how you respond to it. What happens to you is not nearly so important as what you do about it. Events and experiences that challenge your life don't have the last word. They merely represent one opinion. You have a rebuttal to make. You can debate your downside circumstances and argue with the negative in your life. You can have a creative dialogue with problems, challenges, and difficulties. You are never without alternatives, options, and countermoves.

A pastor called on a young man who had recently been serious crippled in a head-on automobile accident.

Expecting the young man to be deeply depressed, the pastor thought about what he might say to him. After a few minutes of small talk, the pastor said to the young man, "An unfortunate accident like yours really colors life, doesn't it?" The young man shifted his broken body in the wheelchair and said to the pastor, "Yes, it does, but I intend to choose the color."

It is not what is taken away from you that is important but what you do with what is left. Pick up the pieces and make a new and better picture with them.

Dear God,
keep teaching me that things turn out
best for those who make the best of the
way things turn out.
Amen.

Listen Up

*Moses said, "The Lord your God will raise
up for you a prophet like me from among your
own people; you must listen to everything he tells you."*
Acts 3:22 NIV

It is still essential that you listen to what is said.
That necessity did not cease when you received a diploma. You will always need to learn, and you will always
learn by listening. Abigail Adams said, "Learning is not
attained by chance. It must be sought for with ardor
and attended to with diligence." If you want to keep
learning, keep listening. There are two kinds of deafness. One comes from a physiological hearing loss and,
other than a hearing aid or perhaps surgery, there's not
much you can do about that. The other deafness comes
from a lack of awareness, from being so preoccupied
with your own agenda that you don't develop or
nurture the skill of listening. You can do something
about that.

Years ago, when people had iceboxes instead of refrigerators, a man working in an ice plant lost a valuable watch in the sawdust in which the ice was stored. His fellow workers searched with him but were unable to find it. They left the plant for lunch and returned to find a young boy with the watch. When they inquired how he found it, he replied, "I just lay down in the sawdust and heard a ticking."

Listening opens whole new worlds populated with fresh ideas, innovative concepts, and illuminating plans.

> *Dear God,*
> *help me listen to hear. Help me hear to*
> *understand. May I understand so*
> *I can make a difference in the*
> *world where I live.*
> *Amen.*

The Promises of God

The world's a huge stockpile of GOD-wonders and God-thoughts. Nothing and no one comes close to you! I start talking abut you, telling what I know, and quickly run out of words. Neither numbers nor words account for you.

Psalm 40:5 MSG

You, being rooted and grounded in love, may be able to comprehend with all the saints what is the breadth and length and height and depth, and to know the love of Christ which surpasses knowledge, that you may be filled up to all the fullness of God.

Ephesians 3:17–19 NASB

The LORD rules over the floodwaters. The LORD reigns as king forever. The LORD gives his people strength. The LORD blesses them with peace.

Psalm 29:10–11 NLT

Every good gift and every perfect gift is from above, and comes down from the Father of lights, with whom there is no variation or shadow of turning.

James 1:17 NKJV

Living the Promises

True happiness, we are told, consists of getting out of one's self, but the point is not only to get out; you must stay out. And to stay out, you must have some absorbing errand.

Henry James

Character cannot be developed in ease and quiet. Only through the experience of trial and suffering can the soul be strengthened, vision cleared, ambition inspired, and success achieved.

Helen Keller

You can learn new things at any time in your life if you're willing to be a beginner. If you actually learn to like being a beginner, the whole world opens up to you.

Barbara Sher

Don't ever tell a young person that something can't be done. God may have been waiting for centuries for somebody ignorant enough of the impossible to do that thing.

J. A. Holmes

Make a Life

You have shown me the path to life, and you make me glad by being near to me. Sitting at your right side, I will always be joyful.

Psalm 16:11 CEV

"Get a life," someone says to another. That means the person being challenged is not living life as it is meant to be experienced, full out with enthusiasm and joy. It means someone is existing on the circumference of life, making too much of too little, instead of moving to the center of life where there is substance, depth, and meaning. Someone is hanging out on the periphery of life, majoring in the minors, and missing the heart of life. To get and have a life means to see life as a gift from God to be experienced richly and fully. It means knowing how blessed you are, and living each day as a response to your blessings. It means taking seriously Jesus' statement that he came to give you abundant life. You go forth from graduation to do more than make a living. You go forth to make a life.

God gives you the threads of talent, interest, curiosity, and skill. Weave a colorful tapestry of truth, value, purpose, and meaning. Make your life a testimony to the goodness of God in it. Show, with your life, how generous God is to you. Receive your life gratefully, embrace it enthusiastically, and use it fully. Don't live only the length of your life. Live its breadth, depth, and height.

The average life span is 25,250 days. Dive all the way down into each one of yours. Don't miss any one of them, or anything they hold for you.

Dear God,
thank you for my life that comes to me
one wonderful day at a time and adds
up to years of possibility and joy.
Amen.

Get Ready

Prepare your work outside, get everything ready for you in the field; and after that build your house.
Proverbs 24:27 NRSV

Self-confidence is a key to success, and preparation is the key to self-confidence. You feel able to do what you have prepared yourself to do. Preparation puts strength in your step and brings victory to your effort. Even when you don't excel with talent, you can win with preparation. More imperative than the will to win is the will to prepare to win. The greatest feeling in the midst of any test life brings comes from knowing you did your homework. You win not by chance but by preparation.

As a young man was planning to make a voyage to England on the *Lusitania*, he heard rumors that the liner might be torpedoed. In preparation for that possibility, he spent time each day in a tub of ice water. He worked up from a few minutes to nearly two hours a day before it was time for the ship to sail. When the

ship was indeed destroyed, a lifeboat picked up this young man after he had been in the frigid ocean for nearly five hours. He was found to be in excellent condition. The preparation he made had saved his life.

Put down on the path of your life the steppingstones of effort, diligence, faithfulness, and thoroughness. Those are the stones that will lead to success.

Your chance will come. Get set for it. Prepare yourself for the opportunities God sends. Get ready today for tomorrow.

Dear God,
I know that when I prepare myself
you give me something special to do and
help me do it.
Amen.

Seven Statements
of Affirmation

I Will...

1. Get out of bed each day thankfully.

2. Be honest about my abilities.

3. Understand how other people can help me.

4. Take time during the day to pray.

5. Believe the biggest room is the one for improvement.

6. Pay attention to life's surprises.

7. Look for the possible in the difficult.

What I Need to Do ...

_____ 1. Read a classic I missed in school.

_____ 2. Spend time with the oldest person I know.

_____ 3. Get a magazine on a subject I know nothing about.

_____ 4. Give my pastor a list of things to pray about for my life.

_____ 5. Ask my parents what makes their life good.

_____ 6. Stop and read a historical marker along the highway.

_____ 7. Call in something positive to a radio talk show.

Choose Well

*Jesus left that place, and as he walked along,
he saw a tax collector, named Matthew, sitting
in his office. He said to him, "Follow me." Matthew
got up and followed him.*

Matthew 9:9 GNT

Your life will be full of choices. Choose wisely,
and choose well. Present choices determine future con-
sequences. Choices, far more than abilities or circumstances, determine who you will be and what you will
accomplish. Choices create conditions and provide
resources. Your choices set the tone for how you live
and make you who you are. Your choices, if good and
sound, will give you a happy and fulfilling life.

The first two chapters of the Bible show that God
gave man and woman a unique status and a distinctive
responsibility. In the way to live life, they had a choice.
As you face life after graduation, so do you. God creates
your choices and presents them to you, but you yourself
must choose. Choose *will* over *won't*, a career over a

job, optimism instead of pessimism. Choose what you want most over what you want now. Select quality over quantity. Choose God. When you choose God, you will have a completely different kind of life. You will have a life filled with direction, encouragement, and faith. You will have someone to help you with all the other choices.

You are in control of your own choices in life. Look at your choices, pick the best one, and then go to work with all your heart.

Dear God,
help me understand my options
and select those that lead me where
you want me to go and where
you want me to be.
Amen.

Show You Care

We were gentle when we were with you,
like a mother taking care of her children.
1 Thessalonians 2:7 GNT

Caring is the key to making your way successfully and meaningfully among the people you will meet in your life. You will find that a sweet spirit of gentle service goes far in smoothing out the wrinkles of human relationships. No one really cares how much you know until it's known how much you really care.

One time a little girl was brought to the office of Carl Jung for the psychiatrist to see. She was not able to speak. Others who had examined her did not think she suffered from neurological or physical illness. Her parents brought her to Jung, and she went into his office and spent an hour with the esteemed doctor. When she came out, she was talking up a storm. Dr. Jung was asked what he had done that enabled the little girl to speak. With a smile warming his countenance, he

explained, "Oh, I just put her up on my lap and sang to her."

You will have many opportunities to put your stamp of caring on those you associate with as you go through life. That is something everybody needs and wants, and you can give it.

Human caring is the most direct channel of divine love. Those you care for know God loves them. When you reach out for them, they are touched by God.

> Dear God,
> thank you for caring for me enough
> to send Jesus Christ to love me.
> May I care for and love others
> as you do me.
> Amen.

79

A Graduate's Prayer

Dear God,
I thank you, O God, the future and its openness,
doors and their keys, roads that lead on,
people who encourage,
and the power of Your promise to be with me.

I thank you, O God, for challenges that test,
failures that teach, jobs to do,
friends to know, and the power of Your
promise to be with me.
Amen.

Thoughts and Promises
for the Journey

A true servant of God is someone
who helps another succeed.

Billy Graham

*God lives in anyone who agrees that Jesus is the Son of God.
That kind of person remains joined to God. So we know that
God loves us. We depend on it.*

1 John 4:15–16 NIrV

Great works do not always lie in our way, but
every moment we may do little ones excellently,
that is, with great love.

Saint Francis de Sales

*Let each of you look not to your own interests,
but to the interests of others.*

Philippians 2:4 NRSV

God has created me to do him some definite
service; he has committed some work to me
which he has not committed to another.

John Henry Newman

Trust Your Heart

Above all else, guard your heart,
for it is the wellspring of life.

Proverbs 4:23 NIV

What you feel in your heart, you think in your head. To know what to do and how to do it, listen to your heart. It is the origin of better thoughts and best instincts. You will have a good life if you consult your heart.

In the course of a political campaign stop, Dwight Eisenhower spoke on the steps of a college campus about the national agenda as he saw it. "We need to become," he told the audience, "a people with an educated heart." You have an educated heart. Your heart knows what to do. It is sensitive, intuitive, and knowledgeable. It has the inside scoop on where you should go and what you should do when you get there. Your heart is filled with instructions and directions that enlighten and illuminate. A group of elementary students was asked to honor one of their teachers by

drawing a picture of something that reminded them of her. One young boy colored an entire page red. When asked to explain, he said, "I wanted to draw a picture of her heart, but her heart is too big for the paper." You have a big heart full of what you need to succeed and bless others.

Your heart is filled with incomparable treasure. It is who you are and where God is. If you want to know how big you are, put the tape measure around your heart.

Dear God,
thank you for living in my heart and
speaking to me from there.
Amen.

The Power of a Smile

Be glad in the LORD and rejoice, O righteous,
and shout for joy, all you upright in heart.
Psalm 32:11 NRSV

When you graduated, you were smiling. Keep it up; it will serve you well. Give your mouth the chance, in all circumstances and on every occasion, to break out into a smile. A smile is a crooked line that straightens out a lot of things. It eases tension, mediates conflict, and chases stress away. It gives warmth, invites joy, relaxes people, and announces you as friend and advocate. It is the shortest distance between two people. A smile is a language everyone understands because it translates itself. It bridges all communication gaps. A smile on your face is the light in the window telling people you are home to them.

Smile when things aren't going well. Smile through the bad times and sad times until you get to the glad times. Swallow what's bitter in the cup, put a

smile on your face, and move on. Smile at the obstacles, laugh at the circumstances, know the joy of being alive. One time, a young girl was reading the story of the wise men from the Bible to her family, and she said, "They presented him gifts of gold, frankincense, and mirth." As you start the rest of your life, take with you the mirth and merriment of a smiling face.

Your smile is more important than anything you wear. When you put a smile on your face, you are fully dressed.

Dear God,
let my smile be a source of delight and
comfort to the people around me.
Amen.

The Promises of God

Your love is a treasure, and everyone finds shelter in the shadow of your wings. You give your guests a feast in your house, and you serve a tasty drink that flows like a river.

Psalm 36:7–8 CEV

Consider yourselves fortunate when all kinds of trials come your way, for you know that when your faith succeeds in facing such trials, the result is the ability to endure.

James 1:2–3 GNT

God is able to make all grace abound to you, so that in all things at all times, having all that you need, you will abound in every good work.

2 Corinthians 9:8 NIV

Bless the LORD, O my soul, and forget none of His benefits; who pardons all your iniquities, who heals all your diseases; who redeems your life from the pit, who crowns you with lovingkindness and compassion; who satisfies your years with good things, so that your youth is renewed like the eagle.

Psalm 103:2–5 NASB

Living the Promises

Occasionally in life there are those moments of
unutterable fulfillment which cannot be completely explained by those symbols called words.
Their meanings can only be articulated by the
inaudible language of the heart.

Martin Luther King Jr.

The higher the ideal, the more work is required
to accomplish it. Do not expect to become a
great success in life if you are not
willing to work for it.

Father Edward Joseph Flanagan

I have always considered life as though it were
a piece of solid granite. You take the chisel of
your willpower and carve the granite. To have a
design ready before you start is as essential as
it is to have a sharp chisel.

Jean Sibelius

Fitness of purpose is one of the most necessary
sinews of character and one of the best instru-
ments of success. Without it, genius wastes its
efforts in a maze of inconsistencies.

Lord Philip Dormer Stanhope Chesterfield

Do It Right

*Strive for the greater gifts. And
I will show you a still more excellent way.*
1 Corinthians 12:31 NRSV

There is no substitute for excellence. Not even success. Do whatever you do the best you can. Aim for the top, go for the record, and you will be widely blessed. Make up your mind right now that your work is going to stand for quality, that you will stamp a superior value on everything that issues from any effort you make. In the Country Music Hall of Fame, there is a plaque that says Loretta Lynn "became a singer because it was the only thing she could do. She became a star because that's the only way she could do it."

Do what you do the right way, the best way. Don't hang around mediocrity. Rise above the ordinary. Remember that average is just as close to the bottom as it is to the top. Honor yourself and God, who made you with excellence. Hoagy Carmichael said of his musical performances, "I don't play anything that's not right.

That way you won't get hostile with yourself." The quality of your life and how you feel about yourself will be in direct proportion to your commitment to excellence, not perfection. Striving for perfection will demoralize you. But striving for excellence will motivate, nurture, and reward you.

Whatever the challenge, whatever the test, whatever you strive for—give it your best. Think only of the best, work only for the best, expect only the best.

Dear God,
help me always to give my best and to
strive for excellence in what I do.
Amen.

More Than Anything

May he give you the desire of your heart
and make all your plans succeed.

Psalm 20:4 NIV

You will achieve your goals if you want to. You will cross the line and get the prize if that is what you desire. Your desire will make you care more than others think is wise, risk more than others think is safe, dream more than others think is practical, and expect more than others think is possible. When your desire is strong, you will have the drive to achieve your objective. Desire gives you strength equal to your wishes.

A professional basketball executive, commenting on why one player exceeded everybody's expectations except his own, said, "They can take a man and measure him, examine him, analyze him, and dissect his statistics, but they can't look into his heart." The player wanted to excel more than anything in the world, and he did better than anyone thought he would. In one game, he scored forty points, had fifteen rebounds, four

steals, and ten assists. At the conclusion of the game, a television commentator said, "He shouldn't be able to do that." His colleague replied, "He wants it more than anybody I've ever seen. That's why he can do it."

The way you undertake your tasks and sustain your undertakings will be determined by your longings and yearnings. You will aim higher and strive longer because you passionately want to reach your goal.

Dear God,
fill my heart with the desire to please
you in all things. May my desire to
please you indeed please you.
Amen.

Seven Statements
of Affirmation

I Will ...

1. Set goals that honor God.

2. Live in a way that shows God to others.

3. Lift others up as I strive toward my goals.

4. Match my desire to my dream.

5. Consult God about what I want.

6. Take responsibility for what I want.

7. Strive for excellence.

What I Need to Do ...

___ 1. Study the Bible each day.

___ 2. Read one inspirational book every month.

___ 3. Interview a successful executive about goal setting.

___ 4. Talk with my parents about my desires.

___ 5. Join a small group that affirms people.

___ 6. Get a hobby that challenges me.

___ 7. Find a younger person to mentor.

The Best Teacher Ever

The first day of school, Mrs. Johnson noticed Tyson Rumfield slumped over in his seat. He looked like that was the last place he wanted to be. She had noticed the year before that he didn't play well with other children on the playground. What would she do with Tyson in her fifth grade class? First thing to do was review his records. His first grade teacher wrote, "Tyson is a bright child who knows how to do many things the other children haven't learned yet." Mrs. Johnson was surprised at this assessment. His second grade teacher wrote, "Tyson is a good student; his classmates like him, but he is troubled because his mom is very sick." His third grade teacher shed more light: "His mother's death devastated Tyson. He can't focus on anything else." The fourth grade teacher confirmed what Mrs. Johnson suspected: "Tyson is completely withdrawn, has no friends, and often sleeps his way through class."

> *I am sending him to you for this very purpose, to let you know how we are, and to encourage your hearts.*
>
> Ephesians 6:22 NRSV

It was Christmastime, and the children had brought presents for their teacher. Mrs. Johnson unwrapped each one. When she got to Tyson's, the class made fun of what he had brought. Mrs. Johnson held up a gemstone necklace with some of the stones missing. She shushed the children and told Tyson how beautiful his present was. She put the necklace on and whirled herself around the room so everyone could see it. She came back to Tyson, bent over, and kissed him on his cheek.

From then on, Mrs. Johnson paid special attention to Tyson. She spent extra minutes with him whenever she had some time. She encouraged him, bragged on him in front of the other children, and found little prizes to give Tyson for work well done. By the end of the school year, Tyson had the highest grades in the class. He was so proud he didn't even mind it when some of the children called him "teacher's pet." The last day of school that year, Mrs. Johnson found a note slid under her door from Tyson. It said, "You're the best teacher I've ever had in my whole life."

Seven years had gone by when Mrs. Johnson got another note from Tyson. It said he had graduated from high school second in his class, and she was still the best teacher he'd ever had in his whole life. Four years after that, a letter came from a downstate university town that said Tyson had graduated from college with the highest of honors. She was still the best teacher he'd ever had, Tyson assured Mrs. Johnson. The letter also said he planned to attend graduate school across the country. He wanted to be a college professor. That day, Mrs. Johnson added tears of joy to those accumulated over the years because of what God had helped her do for Tyson. It seemed a small contribution at the time, but it was paying huge dividends now.

Four years later, Mrs. Johnson received an invitation to attend the graduation ceremony of Tyson E. Rumfield, Ph.D. Since it was thousands of miles away, she couldn't go, but she sent her congratulations along with a leather-bound copy of her favorite classic to Tyson. She inscribed it to "the best student I ever had in my whole life." That spring, there was yet another letter from Tyson. It said he'd met the girl of his dreams and they were going to be married in a nearby city. Would Mrs. Johnson please come to the wedding and sit in the place usually reserved for the mother of the groom?

Of course, she went. Not only that, but she dug out the gemstone necklace with the missing stones Tyson had given her that time for Christmas. She wore it proudly as she was ushered down the aisle to the left side of the church, where she sat in the first seat on the front row. At the reception, she and Tyson squeezed each other in a tight, enduring hug, and Dr. Rumfield said to Mrs. Johnson, "Thank you for making me see what I can do when I really try. I couldn't have done it without you." And then he added, "You're still the best teacher I've ever had in my whole life."

Your investments in others pay huge dividends for them and for you. Your encouragement enlarges everything.

A Graduate's Prayer

Dear God,
As I go on from here, help me say
yes to possibilities and no to temptations,
hello to giving and good-bye to self serving,
yes to many words of hope and no to words of despair,
always to what lifts up and never to what puts down.

As I go on from here, help me be
a light on the hill that shows the way,
a touch on a life that speaks of love,
a look in the eye that offers peace,
a song in the heart that praises you.

As I go on from here, dear God, I know that
you go with me to all places
and are with me in all things.
Amen.

Thoughts and Promises
for the Journey

The best and most beautiful things in
the world cannot be seen or even touched.
They must be felt with the heart.

Helen Keller

*When you are invited, go and sit in the lowest place, so that
your host will come to you and say, "Come on up, my friend, to
a better place." This will bring you honor in the presence of
all the other guests.*

Luke 14:10 GNT

I've always grown from my problems and challenges, from the things that didn't work out.
That's when I've really learned.

Carol Burnett

*Anyone who lives on milk is still a baby. That person does not
want to learn about living a godly life. Solid food is for those who
are grown up. They have trained themselves with a lot of prac-
tice. They can tell the difference between good and evil.*

Hebrews 5:13–14 NIrV

The mediocre teacher tells. The good teacher
explains. The superior teacher demonstrates.
The great teacher inspires.

William Arthur Ward

Wanting to Know

*If any of you is lacking in wisdom, ask God,
who gives to all generously and ungrudgingly,
and it will be given you.*

James 1:5 NRSV

God sends people of wisdom into your life. They are all around. Don't miss them. Some are obvious, others are subtle, and they are all gifts from God to you. Sit at their feet, find out how they think and learn what they know. See what they have seen, listen to what they have heard, sense what they have felt, get their ideas into your head. Follow the advice of Rudyard Kipling, who said, "I keep six honest serving men (they taught me all I knew); their names are What and Why and When and How and Where and Who." Remember that an answer is only an answer for those who are asking a question.

There is nothing more important than asking good questions of those who have the answers. The great playwright Arthur Miller said in a television interview, "As long as my heart beats, my head is going to be

asking questions." He understood the importance of desiring to know enough to find out. It is important for you to ask questions, want to hear answers, understand what is said in response to your queries, and determine to do something about the answers you are given.

Nothing will shape, form, and direct your journey through life any more than the kind of questions you ask. Ask questions whose answers improve your skills, cast light on your path, and fill your heart with the wisdom of God.

Dear God,
thank you for each and every person you
direct into my life to teach, guide, and
direct me. May I not miss any of them.
Amen.

Plunge into Problems

The LORD also will be a stronghold for the oppressed, a stronghold in times of trouble.
Psalm 9:9 NASB

Even with all the positive notes sounded at your graduation, you know there will be difficult times in the life you have ahead of you. Your journey will not be hassle-free. Sometimes you will feel like an extremely small person sent to catch a giant, or someone charged with building a house without hammer and nails. Your life will not always be easy. There will be difficulties. A few of them may be severe, and you'll feel like you're standing barefoot on an anthill. Others will not be so bad, but they will challenge you nevertheless.

The best way out of a difficulty is through it. To try to go around it ignores the problem and allows it to stay right where it is. It is when you go through the dark valley, the psalmist tells us, that you feel the protection of God's rod and staff. It is when you plunge into a problem that you learn to do what you thought

you could not do. It is when you take a pencil and begin connecting the dots that you are able to see the picture. When you start to ascend a mountain, planting step after step, you gain the confidence to accumulate enough steps to get to the top.

When you enter a maze with faith and courage, you will solve its mystery and get to its end. With God at your side, you will handle the hurdles and win the race.

*Dear God,
thank you for difficulties that send me
running to you for the help of your
strength, wisdom, and presence.
Amen.*

The Promises of God

Do not remember the former things, nor consider the things of old. Behold, I will do a new thing, now it shall spring forth; shall you not know it?

Isaiah 43:18–19 NKJV

I am still not all I should be, but I am focusing all my energies on this one thing: Forgetting the past and looking forward to what lies ahead. I strain to reach the end of the race and receive the prize for which God, through Christ Jesus, is calling us up to heaven.

Philippians 3:13–14 NLT

The Lord is not slow to keep his promise. He is not slow in the way some people understand it. He is patient with you. He doesn't want anyone to be destroyed. Instead, he wants all people to turn away from their sins.

2 Peter 3:9 NIrV

Let the mighty strength of the Lord make you strong. Put on all the armor that God gives, so you can defend yourself against the devil's tricks. . . . Let your faith be like a shield, and you will be able to stop all the flaming arrows of the evil one.

Ephesians 6:10–11, 16 CEV

Living the Promises

To me it seems as if when God conceived the world, that was Poetry; He formed it, and that was Sculpture; He colored it, and that was Painting; He peopled it with living beings, and that was the grand, divine, eternal Drama.

Charlotte Cushman

In the time of your life, live—so that in that wondrous time you shall not add to the misery and sorrow of the world, but shall smile to the infinite delight and mystery of it.

William Saroyan

There are three great questions which in life we have over and over again to answer: Is it right or wrong? Is it true or false? Is it beautiful or ugly? Our education ought to help us answer these questions.

John Lubbock

I do not have to make over the universe: I have only to do my job, great or small, and to look often at the trees and the hills and the sky, and be friendly with everyone.

David Grayson

Touch the Fire

He is the source of your life in Christ Jesus, who
became for us wisdom from God, and righteousness and
sanctification and redemption, in order that, as it is
written, "Let the one who boasts, boast in the Lord."

1 Corinthians 1:30–31 NRSV

No matter what you try to do with your life, keep in touch with your source of strength. Stay close to the command station of God's power. When you need support, lean on God. It is in God's mind that you find wisdom for your life. It is in God's heart that you discover the joy and delight of life. Keep the door open to God's presence, and let him keep you company on a daily basis.

When Hercules wrestled with Antaeus, he found that every time he threw his adversary to the ground, he got a stronger foe than the one before. This baffled Hercules until he learned that Earth was the mother of the giant. Every time her son fell upon her bosom, he rose up with renewed strength and greater power.

When he knew the source of his opponent's strength, Hercules changed his strategy. He lifted Antaeus high in the air and held him there away from the source of his strength. Unable to draw from that source, Antaeus was soon defeated. This story reminds you to stay in touch, through prayer, faith, and nurture with God, who is the source of your strength in all things.

If you want a fulfilling life, keep in touch with the fire, because the fire of God's love for you always burns. If you want to get to where you are going, walk with God, who knows the way.

Dear God,
you answer when I call and draw near
to me when I draw near to you.
Wash the high tide of your great
power over my life right now.
Amen.

Send Faith to Answer

*GOD met me more than halfway,
he freed me from my anxious fears.*

Psalm 34:4 MSG

As you go out into the rest of your life, fear will knock on your door many times. It will come to say you cannot do what you set out to do. It will minimize your ability and exaggerate the obstacles that are in your way. When fear knocks at your door, send faith to answer. When faith answers the door on which fear knocks, fear will see the formidable strength that stands there and will turn tail and run. Faith exposes fear for what it is, a hasty conclusion of the mind. Faith lets you know that fears are more numerous than dangers, and that most of your fears are between your ears.

In Bunyan's *Pilgrim's Progress*, Christian travels toward the celestial city, but on the path in front of him is a lion. He remembers the Bible verse about the devil prowling around like a roaring lion, and he quakes with fear. Then he hears a voice say, "Don't be afraid,"

and he walks on. As he gets closer to the lion, he sees the animal is chained and the chain won't let the animal reach the path. As long as Christian walks the middle of the road in faith, he is safe.

When fear knocks at your door, send faith to answer. Fear cannot stand up against faith. Faith is the trump card that takes away every trick from fear.

Dear God,
bring the light of your love to the
darkness of my fears. In you, I
conquer and am victorious.
Amen.

Seven Statements
of Affirmation

I Will ...

1. Be superior to my previous self.

2. Believe I count for something in the world.

3. Understand fear is a feeling, not a fact.

4. Be curious about my environment.

5. Make a habit of doing good deeds.

6. Think as much of myself as God thinks of me.

7. Understand failure is an event, not a person.

What I Need to Do . . .

_____ 1. Create with my hands a symbol of faith.

_____ 2. Put a list of praises on my refrigerator.

_____ 3. At a meeting, sit with someone who usually sits alone.

_____ 4. Affirm the most negative person I know.

_____ 5. Keep a prize box for neighborhood children.

_____ 6. Save my change for missions in a coffee can.

_____ 7. Give a Bible-story book to a child.

Make Up Your Mind

Whatever you decide to do will be accomplished,
and light will shine on the road ahead of you.
Job 22:28 NLT

As you move on from graduation, you will have more decisions to make than you used to have. A lot of what was decided for you by parents and teachers will now be your responsibility. You will sift out options and choose one over the other. You will weigh merit, measure potential, and project consequence. When standing at a fork in the road, which path you take will establish where you arrive and how you get there. Your decisions pave the road of life and take you down it. They are more important than your resources. For instance, Rosa Parks didn't get into history because of her resources. She got there because of her decision. When she decided not to move to the back of the bus, her action spawned the entire civil rights movement.

In the excitement of a high school state basketball tournament, a man with a microphone got hold of the

coach and asked if he was surprised they had won the championship. "No," he said. Going on to explain, he said, "Before the season began, we knew we had the makings of a good team, so the boys and I got together and decided that this year we would go all the way."

What you decide establishes what you have. The selections you make determine the kind of life you live. Good wishes and hopes change little, but good decisions change everything.

Dear God,
be my eternal consultant as I choose
and decide. Help me choose wisely.
Give me strength to make good deci-
sions and abide by them.
Amen.

Make the Effort

You must make every effort to support your faith
with goodness, and goodness with knowledge.

2 Peter 1:5 NRSV

Whatever you attempt, you will do better at it if you keep on trying. You will be much more successful if you continue the effort. Almost anything is possible if you keep working at it. You never lose until you quit trying. As long as you answer the bell for another round, the fight is not over. Don't give up attempting to do what you really want to do. Give the world the best you have, and the best will come back to you.

But your effort is required. God doesn't make orange juice; he makes oranges, and you make orange juice. In the movie *Chariots of Fire*, Harold Abrahams loses a race and sits afterward in the empty stands staring at the track, recalling the pain when his opponent crossed the finish line a fraction of a second ahead of him. Sybil Gordon, his future wife, offers consolation, but Abrahams turns to her and says, "If I can't win, I

won't run." She says to him in counterpoint, "If you don't run, you can't win."

There is a gold mine inside you; make the effort to bring out the gold. Remember, it is not the sugar that makes the tea sweet; it is the stirring. You will know how high is high when you try.

Dear God,
give me hills to climb and the determination
to climb them, races to win and the desire
to win them. May your power
be my strength.
Amen.

A Graduate's Prayer

Dear God,
Help me give a strong effort
and make the best of everything.
Help me make a long run
and leap as high as I can.
Help me remember I am responsible
for the attempt, not the outcome.
Help me do more than is expected
and be glad I did.
Help me add a little to a little
so I can see something big.
Help me give to you what
you will use to bring blessing to all.
Amen.

Thoughts and Promises
for the Journey

I'm just a ballplayer with one ambition,
and that is to give all I've got to help my
ball club win. I've never played any other way.

Joe DiMaggio

Do not throw away your confidence; it will be richly rewarded.
You need to persevere so that when you have done the will of
God, you will receive what he has promised.

Hebrews 10:35–36 NIV

Perseverance is not a long race; it is many
short races one after another.

Walter Elliott

Use common sense and sound judgment! Always keep them in
mind. They will help you to live a long and beautiful life.

Proverbs 3:21–22 CEV

Don't give up trying to do what you really
want to do. Where there is love and inspiration,
I don't think you can go wrong.

Ella Fitzgerald

Go Get It

If any want to become my followers, let them deny them themselves and take up their cross and follow me.
Matthew 16:24 NRSV

If you want something in your life, go get it. Move out from the rationalization of excuses and move on to acquire what you want. Don't depend on others to get it for you. The acquisition of dream and goal is your responsibility.

A man came to America from Eastern Europe and, after being processed at Ellis Island, went into a cafeteria to get something to eat. He sat down at an empty table and waited for someone to take his order. Of course nobody did. Finally, a woman with a tray full of food sat down opposite him and informed him how a cafeteria worked. "Start out at that end," she said, "and go along the line and pick out the food you want. At the other end they'll tell you how much you have to pay."

Later, the man reflected to a new friend on that experience. "I soon learned that's how everything works in America. Life's a cafeteria here. You can get anything you want as long as you are willing to pay the price. But you'll never get what you want if you wait for someone to bring it to you. You have to get up and get it yourself."

You are the only one who can use your ability to reach your goals. You are responsible for moving toward those goals. Your future growth and progress are on your shoulders and in your hands.

Dear God,
thank you for giving me so much and
for so immensely endowing me. I am
grateful for all my blessings.
Amen.

Come to Play

*Being lazy will make you poor,
but hard work will make you rich.*

Proverbs 10:4 GNT

As you set goals for life, if you itch for something, be willing to scratch for it. Make *hard work* your favorite words. Play the game all stops out; hold nothing back. Laziness may appear attractive, but it is work that gives satisfaction and brings results.

John Havlicek was a successful basketball player who was called Mr. Perpetual Motion. Once John Havlicek started running, he didn't stop for sixteen seasons. Packed house or nearly empty arena, crucial game or merely the last one of the season, he gave 100 percent every game. He was talented enough, but it was hustle and hard work that set him apart from other players. That alone would have ensured him the mantle of greatness. John Havlicek was the standard by which other basketball players of his era were measured. Nobody gave a greater effort day in and day out.

Nobody gave all he had every minute of a game, like John Havlicek. He was steady, consistent, and unswerving. Nobody ever gave a greater effort on a basketball court than John Havlicek. He was the very soul of the sports expression "He came to play."

Remember that one thing common to most success stories is the alarm clock. Those who get up early and work hard through the day are rewarded and benefited. Hard work makes for a good life.

Dear God,
as you put Adam and Eve in the
garden to tend and keep it, make my work
a response to the glory of your creation.
Amen.

The Promises of God

I will make an everlasting covenant with them, promising not to stop doing good for them. I will put a desire in their hearts to worship me, and they will never leave me.

Jeremiah 32:40 NLT

You are tempted in the same way all other human beings are. God is faithful. He will not let you be tempted any more than you can take. But when you are tempted, God will give you a way out so that you can stand up under it.

1 Corinthians 10:13 NIrV

My thoughts are not your thoughts, nor are your ways My ways. . . . For as the heavens are higher than the earth, so are My ways higher than your ways and my thoughts than your thoughts.

Isaiah 55:8–9 NASB

This is what love is: It is not that we have loved God, but that he loved us and sent his Son to be the means by which our sins are forgiven.

1 John 4:10 GNT

Living the Promises

The only way to live is to accept each minute as an unrepeatable miracle, which is exactly what it is—a miracle and unrepeatable.

Margaret Storm Jameson

Without enthusiasm you are doomed to a life of mediocrity, but with it you can accomplish miracles.

Og Mandino

I do not try to dance better than anyone else. I only try to dance better than myself.

Mikhail Baryshnikov

Nothing of great value in life comes easily.

Norman Vincent Peale

I do not know anyone who reached the top without hard work. That's the recipe. It will not always get you to the top but should get you pretty near.

Margaret Thatcher

The Best Word

*Since we are receiving a kingdom that cannot be
shaken, let us be thankful, and so worship God
acceptably with reverence and awe.*

Hebrews 12:28 NIV

The best word to remember as you go through life
is *thanks*. Be aware of your many blessings and the
great variety of creative ways God gives them to you.
Be grateful for everything. A Vietnamese proverb says,
"When eating fruit, think of the person who planted
the tree." Go through life with a great sense of wonder
and gratitude for everything. Give thanks for each and
every gift you receive. Be always aware of the wonderful bounty of your life.

There is a woman who has formed the habit of
writing "Thanks" on the lower left-hand corner of
every check she writes. When she pays her gas bill or
water bill, she expresses her gratitude to those who
make their services available to her at the push of a but-
ton. She writes of her thankfulness to the young man

from around the corner who mows her lawn, and the baker who makes her bread and cookies. Gratitude for all things lives in her heart because she never fails to count her many blessings.

Gratitude is the heart's memory of the blessings of God. When you know the language of gratitude, you will always be on speaking terms with joy and peace. All things are beautiful when they are seen as gifts.

Dear God,
my prayer is always one of gratitude.
I thank you for this day, those
I will be with in it, and for
your presence at all times.
Amen.

Believe It Will Work

Without faith it is impossible to please God, because anyone who comes to him must believe that he exists and that he rewards those who earnestly seek him.

Hebrews 11:6 NIV

Believe in your ideas, and have faith to put them to work. You will achieve if you believe. Think you can, and you will. Rudyard Kipling said, "First prizes don't always go to the brightest and strongest; again and again the person who wins is the one who is sure he can."

The owner of a hardware store had numerous items he could not sell. A young boy who worked for the merchant had an idea he believed in. "Why don't we put all the unsold merchandise on a table out on the sidewalk and stick up a sign that says, 'ten cents or less—take your choice'?" The owner tried to put down the boy's idea but the boy insisted it would work, and the merchant finally let him try it. In no time, everything was sold. "Let's try it again," the boy said, but

nothing he could do persuaded his boss to let him do it again. So the boy quit his job and started his own business. He called it "a five-and-ten-cent store." Years later, F. W. Woolworth became one of the most successful merchandisers in history.

Believe you can accomplish something, and you will find the capacity to do it. You can because you believe you can. Success and happiness come when you believe in yourself enough to keep on trying.

*Dear God,
when I think about how much you love
and bless me, I have confidence to
stand up and move forward.
Amen.*